GIANTS OF THE JURASSIC

by Louise Nelson

Minneapolis, Minnesota

Credits: All images are courtesy of Shutterstock.com, unless otherwise specified. With thanks to Getty Images, Thinkstock Photo, and iStockphoto. Cover – Warpaint, Julia-art, Vac1, Natali Snailcat, Nikulina Tatiana, Trifonenkolvan, Dotted Yeti. Images used on every page – Julia-art, Natali Snailca, Nikulina Tatiana, Trifonenkolvan. 2 – Daniel Eskridge. 4–5 – Catmando, Dotted Yeti, Orla. 6–7 – Dotted Yeti. 8–9 – Daniel Eskridge. 10–11 – racksuz, Sk_Advance studio. 12–13 – Michael Rosskothen, Sk_Advance studio. 14–15 – Daniel Eskridge, Michael Rosskothen, Sk_Advance studio. 16–17 – Dariush M, Esteban De Armas, Sk_Advance studio. 18–19 – Diego Fiore, Lost_in_the_Midwest. 20–21 – paleontologist natural, YuRi Photolife. 22–23 – Russ Heinl, Tenebroso.

Library of Congress Cataloging-in-Publication Data is available at www.loc.gov or upon request from the publisher.

ISBN: 979-8-88509-364-4 (hardcover)
ISBN: 979-8-88509-486-3 (paperback)
ISBN: 979-8-88509-601-0 (ebook)

© 2023 Booklife Publishing
This edition is published by arrangement with Booklife Publishing.

North American adaptations © 2023 Bearport Publishing Company. All rights reserved. No part of this publication may be reproduced in whole or in part, stored in any retrieval system, or transmitted in any form or by any means, electronic, mechanical, photocopying, recording, or otherwise, without written permission from the publisher.

For more information, write to Bearport Publishing, 5357 Penn Avenue South, Minneapolis, MN 55419.

CONTENTS

The Time of Dinosaurs 4
The Jurassic Period 6
Dinosaurs of the Jurassic 8
Not a Dino 10
How Do We Know? 12
Pliosaurus 14
Liopleurodon 16
Dimorphodon 18
Pterodactyl 20
End of the Jurassic 22
Glossary 24
Index 24

THE TIME OF DINOSAURS

Triassic

Long, long ago, very different creatures wandered Earth. Some had big bodies, terrifying teeth, or terrific tails. They were dinosaurs!

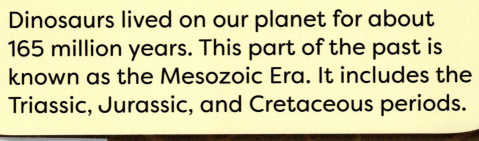

Dinosaurs lived on our planet for about 165 million years. This part of the past is known as the Mesozoic Era. It includes the Triassic, Jurassic, and Cretaceous periods.

Jurassic

Cretaceous

Different dinos lived during different periods.

THE JURASSIC PERIOD

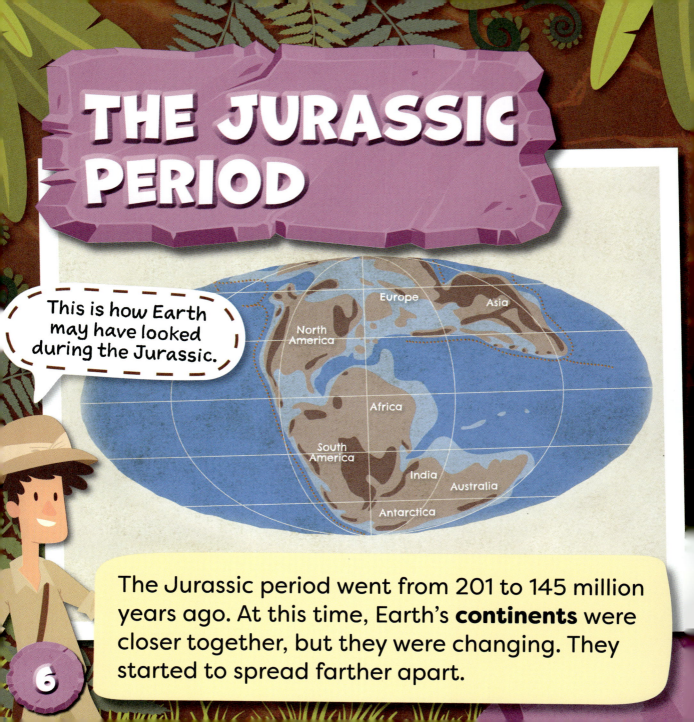

This is how Earth may have looked during the Jurassic.

The Jurassic period went from 201 to 145 million years ago. At this time, Earth's **continents** were closer together, but they were changing. They started to spread farther apart.

As the continents moved, mountains began to form. Water began to rise, creating seas. Many birds and small ocean creatures first showed up during this period.

DINOSAURS OF THE JURASSIC

Brachiosaurus

The Jurassic period is sometimes called the golden age of dinosaurs. During this time, some dinos **evolved** to become **gigantic**.

Allosauruses

Stegosaurus

Allosaurus was a **predator**. It may have hunted huge dinosaurs.

Some dinos had bones like **armor** on their bodies. These bones helped keep them safe.

NOT A DINO

Many dinosaurs lived during the Jurassic period. But other creatures did, too.

Dinosaurs are a specific group of animals. All dinosaurs are **reptiles**. Their legs come out from right under their bodies.

HOW DO WE KNOW?

Old bones called **fossils** give us clues to the past. Scientists called **paleontologists** (*pale*-ee-uhn-TOL-uh-jists) study them.

Paleontologists can use fossils to learn what an animal looked like or how it may have acted. Whose bones have they found?

PLIOSAURUS
(PLY-oh-SORE-us)

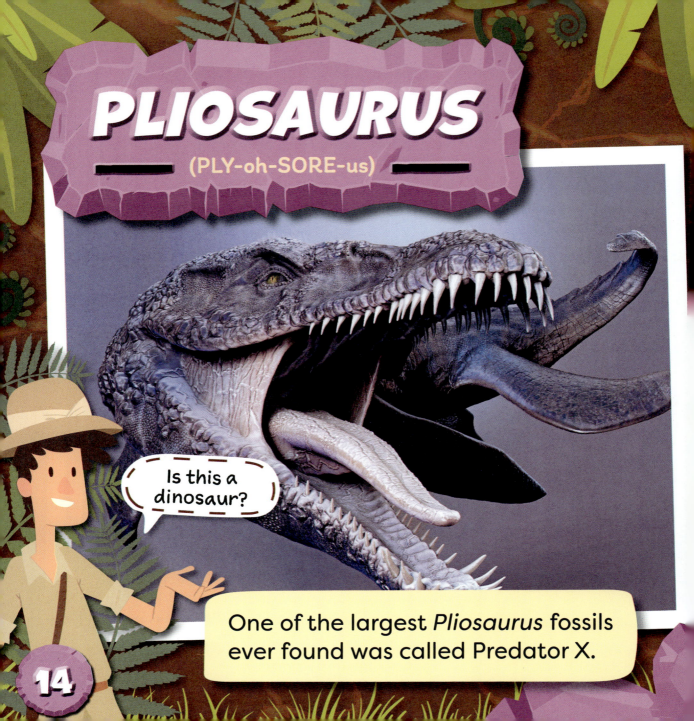

Is this a dinosaur?

One of the largest *Pliosaurus* fossils ever found was called Predator X.

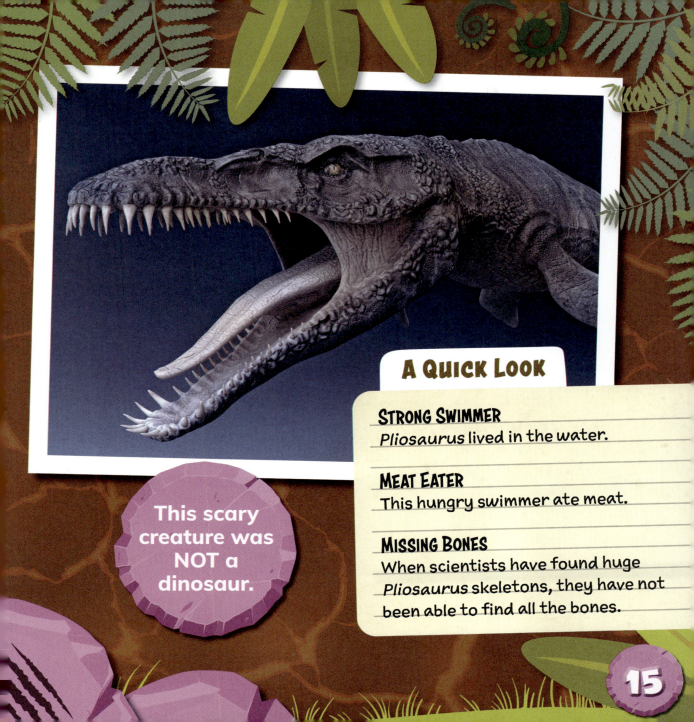

This scary creature was NOT a dinosaur.

A Quick Look

Strong Swimmer
Pliosaurus lived in the water.

Meat Eater
This hungry swimmer ate meat.

Missing Bones
When scientists have found huge *Pliosaurus* skeletons, they have not been able to find all the bones.

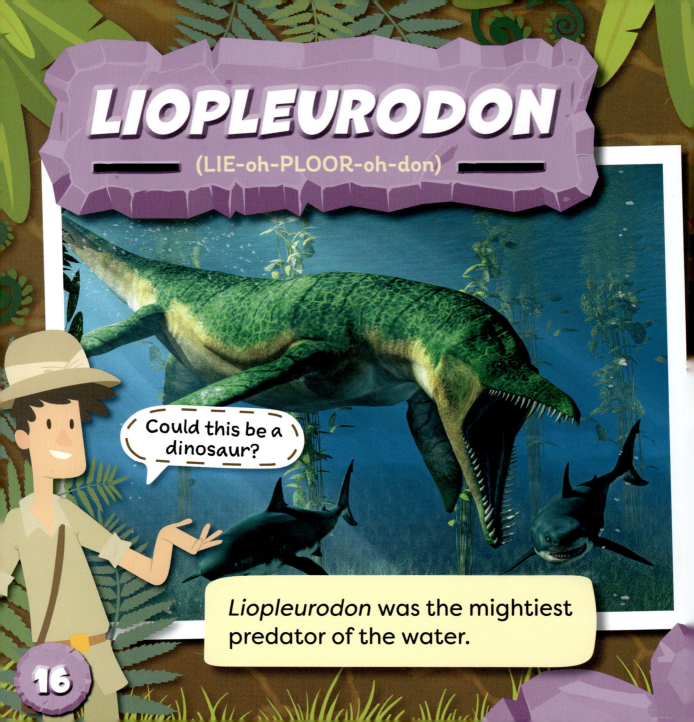

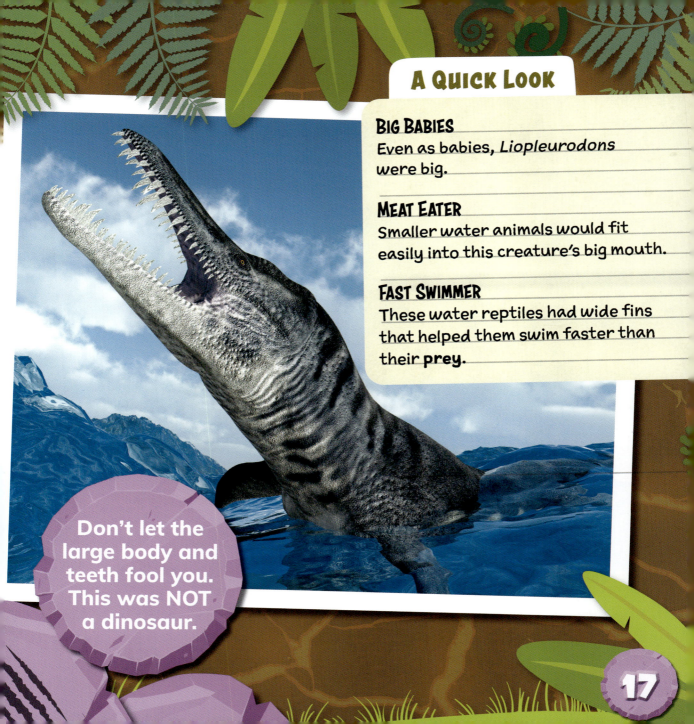

A Quick Look

Big Babies
Even as babies, *Liopleurodons* were big.

Meat Eater
Smaller water animals would fit easily into this creature's big mouth.

Fast Swimmer
These water reptiles had wide fins that helped them swim faster than their **prey.**

Don't let the large body and teeth fool you. This was NOT a dinosaur.

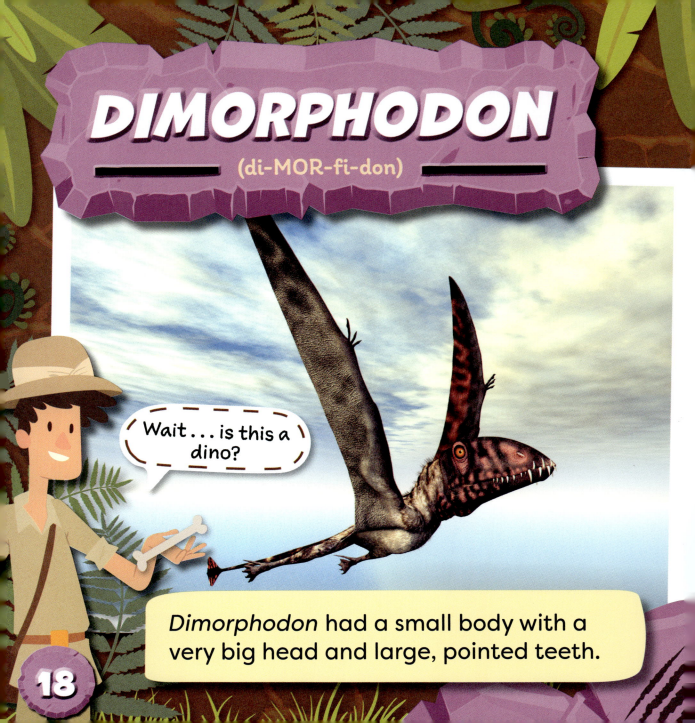

A Quick Look

By Wing or By Foot
Dimorphodon had wings, but it may have walked around on two legs.

Meat Eater
This reptile ate insects. It may have eaten fish, too.

Long Tail
This small creature had a very long tail.

Although some dinos were small, this toothy creature was NOT a dinosaur.

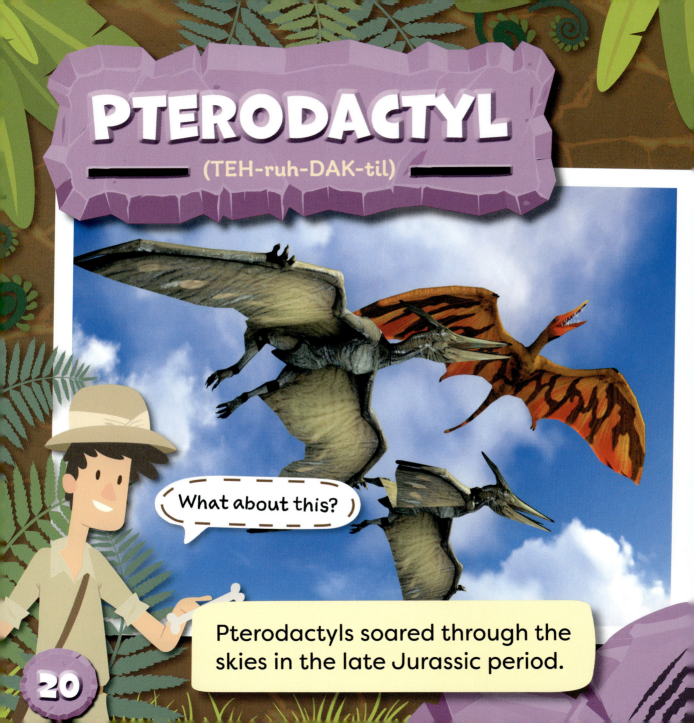

Pterodactyl is well known, but this flying creature was NOT a dinosaur.

A Quick Look

Flying Reptile
Some scientists think a pterodactyl's wings connected its front and back legs.

Meat Eater
This creature might have swooped down from above to catch its prey.

Not a Pterodactyl?
Because the pterodactyl was the first flying reptile found, people sometimes use this name for all creatures that took to the skies during this time.

END OF THE JURASSIC

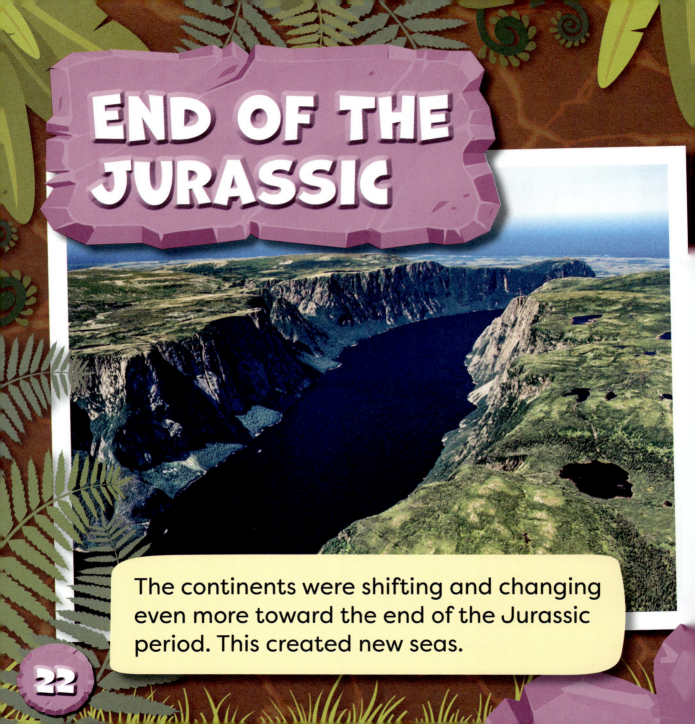

The continents were shifting and changing even more toward the end of the Jurassic period. This created new seas.

The animals were changing, too. Some creatures began to die out, but many dinosaurs and large reptiles continued to rule Earth into the Cretaceous period.

GLOSSARY

armor hard coverings that protect the body

continents the world's seven largest land masses

evolved changed slowly and naturally over time

fossils bones, teeth, or other things left behind from life long ago

gigantic very large

paleontologists scientists who study fossils to find out about life in the past

predator an animal that hunts and kills other animals for food

prey an animal that is hunted for food

reptiles cold-blooded animals that breathe air and have scaly skin

INDEX

armor 9
bones 9, 11–13, 15
continents 6–7, 22
fins 17
fossils 12–14
Mesozoic Era 5
paleontologists 12–13
reptiles 10–11, 17, 19, 21, 23
water 7, 15–17
wings 19, 21